CEREMONIES and RITUALS

DEATH

BY JOANNA BRUNDLE

©2018
Book Life
King's Lynn
Norfolk PE30 4LS

ISBN: 978-1-78637-262-8

Written by:
Joanna Brundle

Edited by:
Kirsty Holmes

Designed by:
Daniel Scase

A catalogue record for this book
is available from the British Library.

CONTENTS

Page 4   **Introduction**

Page 6   **Ancient Death Rituals**

Page 8   **Judaism**

Page 12   **Christianity**

Page 16   **Islam**

Page 20   **Hinduism**

Page 24   **Sikhism**

Page 28   **Buddhism**

Page 31   **Glossary**

Page 32   **Index**

Words that look like **THIS** are explained in the glossary on page 31.

INTRODUCTION

Death is part of the journey of life. It comes to every living thing, from humans and other animals to flowers and flies. But what is death? Is it simply the end of the journey or is it the beginning of a new one? People have very different ideas about this, but nobody knows for sure what actually happens to us after we die. What we do know is that death is a time of great sadness for relatives and friends of a loved one who has died.

A family visits the **GRAVE** of a loved one.

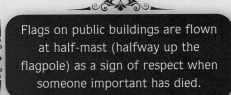

Flags on public buildings are flown at half-mast (halfway up the flagpole) as a sign of respect when someone important has died.

Rituals and ceremonies which honour the dead and prepare them for possible life after death have existed for centuries. People turn to their religion and to the **CUSTOMS** and **TRADITIONS** of their culture to support, comfort and guide them. In this book, we shall be reading about death ceremonies and rituals from around the world, looking especially at the world's major religions and some ancient civilisations.

DIA DE LOS MUERTOS (DAY OF THE DEAD)

Dia de Los Muertos takes place every year in Mexico, and other countries including Spain and Brazil. People honour the memory of dead relatives, believing that their **SOULS** are briefly released from heaven and allowed to return home. Children are remembered on the 1st of November. Adults are remembered on the 2nd of November.

A DECORATED OFRENDA

People clean their loved one's grave and leave offerings of food and drink, including a sweet bread called pan de muerto. The dough is made into the shape of bones. Small **ALTARS** called ofrendas are set up at home. These are decorated with photographs, candles, marigolds and sugar skulls called calaveras. Bedding is also set out for the souls to use after their journey home.

Although Dia de Los Muertos sounds like a sad occasion, it is actually a joyful celebration of the lives of those who have died.

Marigolds are known as the 'flores de muerto', or the 'flowers of the dead'. They are carried in processions and placed on graves and altars because they are believed to attract the souls of the dead.

People dress up for Day of the Dead processions in skull masks or makeup, and try to wake the dead by rattling shells and ringing bells.

The tomb of Muhammad is beneath the green dome.

PLACES OF PILGRIMAGE

Pilgrims are people who travel to **SACRED** places for religious reasons. The **TOMBS** of saints and religious leaders often become places of pilgrimage. Every year, millions of Muslims visit the tomb of the **PROPHET** Muhammad at Medina in Saudi Arabia.

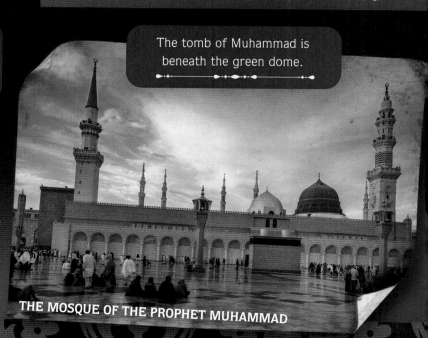

THE MOSQUE OF THE PROPHET MUHAMMAD

THE ANCIENT EGYPTIANS

The Ancient Egyptians believed that life continued after death, in the afterlife.
It was therefore very important that the body was PRESERVED after death. They EMBALMED or mummified the body to preserve it. The ORGANS were removed and the body was covered in a type of salt to dry it out. After 40 days, it was stuffed with sand. After 70 days, it was covered in bandages and placed in a SARCOPHAGUS, before being buried in a tomb. Important, wealthy people had a death mask to guard them from evil spirits. Items that the dead person might need in the afterlife, such as furniture and tools, were buried with them.

The Egyptians believed that the soul returned to the body after death and that the death mask would help the soul to recognise the body.

The eye of the sky god, Horus, was believed to protect anything behind it. AMULETS showing the eye were often placed on the sarcophagus.

THE AFTERLIFE

The Egyptians believed that Osiris, the god of rebirth, judged people's souls in the afterlife. The heart was always left in the dead person's body because the Egyptians believed it was weighed against the Feather of Truth, before the person could reach the afterlife. If it was heavy with SIN, the person's heart and soul were eaten by the monster Ammit.

The Feather of Truth was the symbol of Ma'at, the goddess of truth and justice.

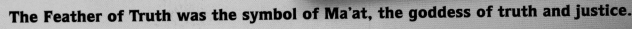

THE ANCIENT GREEKS

The Ancient Greeks washed and **ANOINTED** the body before placing a circular **WREATH** on it. The shape symbolised the circle of eternal life and wreaths are still often placed on a **COFFIN** for the same reason. A coin was placed in the mouth of the dead person. This was to pay Charon, the ferryman who took souls across the River Styx to Hades, the land of the dead.

The Greeks and Romans mostly buried their dead outside their city walls. Burial inside the city walls was reserved for the most important citizens, such as Roman emperors.

THE TERRACOTTA ARMY

The Terracotta Army is a collection of around 8,000 life-sized sculptures of the armies of Qin Shi Huang, the first emperor of China (259–210 BC). The figures were buried with him around his tomb in 210–209 BC and were part of a huge necropolis, or burial complex. The warriors were intended to protect the emperor in the afterlife and to help him to keep order. Sculptures of chariots and horses were also found, along with acrobats and musicians to provide entertainment! The warriors are precisely arranged according to their rank and were originally painted to make them look even more life-like.

The Terracotta Army was discovered by accident in 1974 by Chinese farmers digging a water well.

JUDAISM

Followers of Judaism are called Jews. Different forms of the religion exist around the world, but they all have similar death ceremonies and rituals. Jews believe that, after death, the body should be allowed to return to the earth.

TALLIT

> The practice of embalming is not allowed in Judaism.

PREPARATIONS FOR BURIAL

Traditionally, a Jew's last spoken words should be a prayer of thanksgiving and faith, called the Shema. The dying person says the prayer after **CONFESSING** their sins. After death, the body is prepared for burial. This task may be carried out by members of the Chevra Kaddisha, or holy society. These volunteers make sure the body is properly cared for until burial. The body is washed in warm water and is wrapped in simple white **SHROUDS**.

Jews are buried in their prayer shawl or tallit. To symbolise the fact that the dead person can no longer use the tallit, one of the tassels is removed before burial.

> Jewish shrouds, called tachrichim, are the same for every Jew, symbolising that everyone is equal in God's eyes. The shroud is made up of 10 pieces of cloth for a man and 12 for a woman.

Someone sits with the body at all times until the burial. The Chevra Kaddisha may organise this, especially for someone who has no family of their own. People sitting with the body must show complete respect and are not allowed to eat or drink. They may read from the **BOOK OF PSALMS**, used in Jewish worship.

THE FUNERAL AND BURIAL

The closest relative of the dead person must make sure that the funeral, or levoyah, and burial are arranged as soon as possible. This is usually within a day of the death, but burials are not allowed on the **SABBATH**.

In Israel, Jews are usually buried without a coffin. In other countries, simple wooden coffins that decay easily are used. The funeral itself is a simple ceremony, during which a **RABBI** gives a blessing and recites prayers and psalms.

The ceremony can take place at the synagogue (Jewish temple) or beside the grave.

Close relatives make a small tear in their clothing or in a piece of black ribbon. The tear symbolises their sorrow. The shrouded body or coffin is carried to a Jewish cemetery, usually by male members of the family. They may stop seven times on the way. Each time, they recite part of Psalm 91, from the Book of Psalms, which calls upon the angels to guard the dead person. **MOURNERS** throw soil onto the coffin or shroud when it is in the ground.

Members of the Chevra Kaddisha ensure that every Jew has a dignified funeral and burial, even if they have no family or money.

This Jewish funeral has taken place in a cemetery in Jerusalem, Israel.

AFTER THE BURIAL

Mourners wash their hands after the burial and then gather for a meal known as seudat havra'ah, the meal of comfort. This meal traditionally includes lentil stew and round-shaped foods, such as peeled hard-boiled eggs and bagels, that symbolise the never-ending circle of life.

JEWISH MOURNING

Close relatives of the dead person observe a seven–day period of mourning. This is called sitting Shiva. The day of the funeral is the first day. During the week of Shiva, a candle burns continuously. Each day, an adult mourner says a special prayer, known as the Kaddish, and the rabbi calls to hold an evening service with the family.

Jews traditionally wear their funeral clothes for the week of Shiva.

After three days, visitors are allowed to call. They care for the family and bring Shiva trays or baskets which contain food, including cooked meats, dried fruit and chocolate. Mourners go back to their work after one month but continue to say the Kaddish each day. After eleven months, life goes back to normal. Within the first year, the family arranges for a GRAVESTONE to be erected.

THE ANNIVERSARY OF THE DEATH

The anniversary – the date each year – of the death of a loved one is known as yahrzeit. A special candle, called a yahrzeit candle, is lit at sundown. It burns continuously for 25 hours. The family remembers their loved one and prayers may be said. The candle flame symbolises the human soul.

A YAHRZEIT CANDLE

Traditionally, relatives visit the grave and the synagogue. Some synagogues have a wall of **PLAQUES** to remember and show respect to the dead. Jewish people often leave a stone at the grave, rather than flowers. Unlike flowers, which quickly decay, stones are permanent and symbolise lasting memories of the dead person.

Do you think there is an afterlife? Ask other people about their ideas. Remember that nobody can be certain about this.

THE AFTERLIFE

Jewish people believe that death is only a step in the journey of life. A dead person's body returns to the earth but their soul is believed to return to God in the afterlife. Jews call this afterlife Olam Ha–Ba, meaning 'world to come'. But Judaism also concentrates on the importance of living life well in this world, the Olam Ha–Zeh.

STONES LEFT AT A JEWISH GRAVE

CHRISTIANITY

Across the world, Christianity exists in many forms, or denominations, but they all share the same basic values and beliefs. Christians believe in eternal life after death and that the soul passes to heaven or hell.

Statues of angels are sometimes used on tombstones to symbolise heaven.

THE LAST RITES

Priests often visit dying people and their families, either at home or in hospital, to pray with them and to offer support. The priest may offer a dying person the **LAST RITES**, which gives the person the chance to say sorry for the sins they have committed in their life. This is called repentance. Prayers and a blessing are said and the person may take Holy Communion, also known as the Eucharist. They are given bread (usually in the form of a wafer) and wine by the priest, symbolising the body and blood of Jesus.

Christians take Holy Communion in memory of Jesus and his sacrifice on the cross.

ARRANGEMENTS FOR THE FUNERAL

Until the funeral, the body of a dead person is cared for by an **UNDERTAKER** at a funeral home. The body is embalmed and is usually dressed in the person's best or favourite clothes. The embalmed body is then placed in a coffin in a sacred space, called a chapel of rest, until the funeral.

Family members and friends can visit the funeral home to say their final goodbye to their loved one. The undertaker talks about the funeral with the **BEREAVED** family and makes all the necessary arrangements.

Modern embalming methods use chemicals including methanol, a type of alcohol, to preserve the body.

THE FUNERAL

Christian funerals take place at a church. The funeral usually takes place a few days or weeks after the person's death. At the funeral a Psalm from the Bible is read out. This is usually Psalm 23, the Lord is my shepherd. After the funeral the body is buried and the priest will say, "we commit this body to the ground, earth to earth, ashes to ashes, dust to dust."

THE SERVICE

It is common to feel very sad at a funeral service, but a Christian funeral also gives mourners the chance to celebrate and give thanks to God for the deceased's life. Mourners are comforted by the promise of eternal life. The service includes hymns, readings and prayers, including the **LORD'S PRAYER**. Families remember the life of their relative and their good deeds with a **EULOGY**, which might include the person's favourite poetry and music.

> The coffin is usually closed for the funeral and is often decorated with flowers. Special items, such as a teddy bear for a child or a soldier's cap, may be placed inside or on top of the coffin.

AFTER THE FUNERAL

The coffin is carried into and out of church by pall bearers, who are often relatives and friends of the deceased.

The priest reads these words from the gospel of John in the New Testament of the Bible: "he that believes in me, though he were dead, yet shall he live: and whoever lives and believes in me shall never die."

The coffin is buried in the church graveyard or cemetery. A gravestone to mark the grave is usually erected by the family later. The stone is engraved with the person's name, their dates of birth and death and usually with an **EPITAPH**. If there has been a cremation, the ashes may be buried later in the churchyard or crematorium garden. Some people choose to scatter the ashes somewhere that was special to the dead person.

THE RESURRECTION

Christians believe that although Jesus died on the cross, he came back to life in the Resurrection, celebrated at Easter. They believe that Jesus died to forgive the sins of ordinary people. His resurrection gives Christians hope of eternal life. Repentance of sin allows a person's soul to reach the paradise of heaven.

The sign of the cross is often used for gravestones to symbolise the Resurrection and the promise of eternal life. Funeral flowers are also used.

QUEEN VICTORIA

MOURNING

Christianity does not have a set period of time for mourning. The way in which people mourn and for how long is their own decision. In the UK in the 19th century, however, mourning followed strict guidelines. Families followed the example of Queen Victoria who, after her husband Prince Albert died, avoided social gatherings and wore black clothes. Mourning jewellery was made of jet, a black coal-like material. Widows, wives who have lost their husbands, were expected to mourn for two years.

Although dark colours are still worn at most funerals, mourners sometimes wear brightly coloured clothes to celebrate the life of the dead person.

It was considered bad luck to keep mourning clothes, so new black garments had to be bought for each death.

ISLAM

Followers of Islam, called Muslims, believe that peace comes from obedience to the will of Allah. Death must be accepted as part of God's will, because only Allah gives and takes away life. The Hadith, the teachings of the prophet Muhammad, gives Muslims guidance on funeral rites and preparations for the afterlife.

 Allah is the Muslim word for God.

The family gathered around a dying person must ensure that the last words spoken or heard by them are the first words that they heard as a baby: 'There is no God but Allah and Muhammad is his messenger'. This is called the Shahadah and is the declaration of faith.

YOUNG MUSLIM WOMAN READING THE HADITH

PREPARATIONS FOR BURIAL

The eyes are gently closed and the body is then ritually washed by a person of the same gender, ideally a close relative. A spice called camphor is sometimes used to anoint the body. The body is then wrapped in simple white shrouds. Men are usually wrapped in three sheets, like Muhammad. Women are wrapped in five or seven sheets. Muslims must be buried as soon as possible after death, ideally within 24 hours. Cremation is not allowed because Muslims believe that the body was given by Allah and must be returned to him.

A MUSLIM TOMB STONE

The simple shroud, known as a kafan, symbolises that all people are equal in God's eyes.

THE FUNERAL AND BURIAL

Muslim funerals are very simple. After the body has been prepared, the **IMAM** says prayers, often at the home of the dead person. The shrouded body is then carried to the cemetery on the shoulders of mourners, who usually wear white. The mourners take turns, four at a time, to carry the body. The funeral procession is quiet and mourners are expected not to cry. This shows respect for the dead person and that they accept Allah's will. Traditionally, the body is buried without a coffin, so that it is returned quickly to Allah.

These mourners are all taking turns to carry the body.

At the place of burial, the imam stands behind the shrouded body, facing the holy city of Makkah, sometimes called Mecca. The mourners form rows behind him, all facing Makkah. Muslims usually pray with the knees, toes, palms, forehead and nose touching the floor, but prayers at the graveside are always said standing up. The body is buried on its right side, facing Makkah.

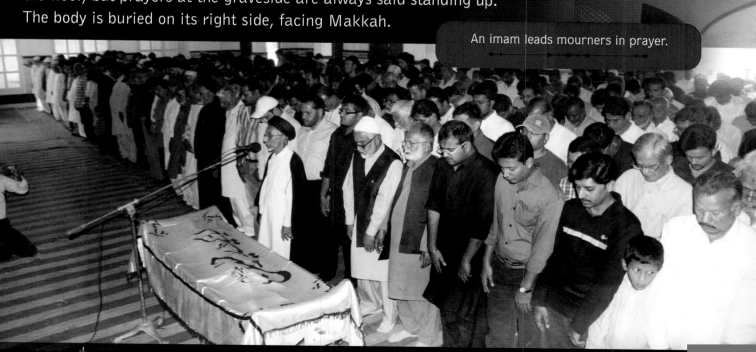

An imam leads mourners in prayer.

AFTER THE BURIAL

After the burial, Muslims observe a period of mourning for three days and nights. Friends call at the home of the bereaved family, to bring food and to offer comfort and support. They encourage the family to accept the death as Allah's will. Prayers are said constantly during the mourning period. A widow mourns her husband for four months and ten days. During this time, known as Iddah, she is not allowed to wear perfume or jewellery and can only leave the house for work or household errands.

Borrowing money and being in DEBT are discouraged in Muslim culture. It is a matter of honour that any debts left by the deceased must be paid off in full by the family.

MUSLIM CEMETERIES

The family of the deceased arranges for a gravestone to be erected. Like Muslim funerals, Muslim cemeteries are very simple, with plain white gravestones. A Muslim grave is usually  raised above ground level, so that the place of burial is clearly marked and nobody walks on it accidentally. No flowers, candles or offerings are left at the graveside.

The symbol of Islam, the star and crescent, is often seen on gravestones.

Can you see the star and crescent on the gravestone at the front?

It is customary for Muslim families to visit the graves of loved ones during the festival of Eid or Eid ul-Fitr, at the end of RAMADAN.

THE DAY OF JUDGEMENT

Muslims believe in eternal life after death, in heaven or hell. They believe that all people will eventually face the Day of Judgement, when their actions on Earth will be judged.

The time between death and the Day of Judgement is known as barzakh.

Two angels, called Munkar and Nakir, are believed to be watching over people throughout their lives. They record good and bad deeds for the Day of Judgement. The angel Israfil will announce the Day of Judgement by blowing his trumpet. Those who have led a blameless life will live forever in paradise. It is depicted in the Qur'an as a beautiful flower garden, symbolising the joy of living with Allah forever. Those who have been sinful will go to hell, suffering the pain of separation from Allah's presence forever.

The Qur'an is the holy book of Islam.

The angel Ridwan is the guardian of paradise. Malik is the guardian of hell.

Once a person has died, they cannot be forgiven for their sins, even if prayers are said for them.

THE FIVE PILLARS OF ISLAM

The five pillars – or beliefs – of Islam are that Muslims should affirm their faith daily, pray five times a day, help the poor, fast during Ramadan and go on Hajj, a pilgrimage to Makkah. Muslims believe that living in this way will allow them to enter paradise.

HINDUISM

The life of a Hindu is marked by 16 rites of passage, known as samskars. Hindus believe it is their religious duty to follow the rituals and ceremonies of each one. The Antima samskar is performed by the family of the dead person. When a Hindu is close to death, the family gathers together. They chant MANTRAS and say prayers from the Vedas, the Hindu holy scriptures.

Married Hindu women are often cremated wearing the mangala sutra necklace, given to them on their wedding day.

A MANGALA SUTRA NECKLACE

PREPARING THE BODY FOR CREMATION

Traditionally, the body is prepared for burial by close family members. It is washed in a mixture of yoghurt, milk, honey and ghee (a type of butter). The palms of the hands are placed together, as if the person is praying, and the big toes are tied together. The body is then traditionally dressed in new white clothes.

The body is then placed on a grass mat and, if possible, a few drops of water from the River Ganges are sprinkled on the head. The body is placed with the head facing south because Yama, the Hindu god of the dead, is thought to come from this direction. Sweet-smelling spices and garlands of brightly coloured flowers such as marigolds are arranged around the body.

THE CREMATION

Hindus believe that, after death, the soul leaves the body. Cremation is believed to release the soul quickly and the body is cremated as soon as possible after death. In India, the body is tied to a bamboo stretcher, known as a bier, and is carried to the cremation site. People in the funeral procession may play drums and horns. In urban areas and western countries, the body is cremated at a crematorium and is taken there in a hearse.

The body is carried to the burial site on a bamboo stretcher.

The only Hindus who are buried rather than cremated are those considered to be pure – very young children and holy men and women.

THE CREMATION

The chosen site is usually beside a river, particularly the sacred River Ganges. It is **PURIFIED** with water and evil spirits are scared away with chanting. A funeral **PYRE** is built from logs on ghats (steps) along the river banks. The body is placed on top of the pyre. If the deceased has an eldest son, he walks around the pyre three times, in an anti-clockwise direction, before lighting it. Prayers are offered to Agni, the fire god. Ghee is thrown onto the fire.

A FUNERAL PYRE ON THE BANKS OF THE SACRED RIVER BAGHMATI IN NEPAL

AFTER THE CREMATION

After the fire has died down, the mourners return home, led by the youngest male mourner. They go through a purification process, including washing, changing their clothes and symbolically touching fire, stone and oil. A period of mourning lasting 11 or 13 days follows the cremation. During this time, the family does not take part in any festivals or other social gatherings and is considered to be unclean. Cooking is banned, so neighbours and friends provide food, as well as support.

Hindu mourners in Nepal comfort one another.

After three days, the ashes are collected and are scattered, ideally in the River Ganges or another sacred river. Ashes from a crematorium are also scattered in this way. Families living outside India try to make the journey to the River Ganges to scatter the ashes. The family marks the anniversary of the death by offering balls of rice, called pindas, to the poor.

Hindu widows traditionally wear a plain white SARI, with no jewellery.

The end of mourning is marked by the kriya ceremony in which a Hindu priest, known as a Brahmin, blesses the house of the dead person.

REINCARNATION

Hindus believe in reincarnation. This means, after death, the soul is reborn many times into new bodies, in a continual circle of life – birth, old age, death and rebirth. This circle is known as Samsara. The circle is broken only when the soul joins Brahman, the one true god, by achieving purity and wisdom. This freedom from Samsara is known as moksha.

The Bhagavad Gita, the Hindu holy book, likens the journey of the soul to taking off old clothes and replacing them with new ones.

THE SACRED CITY OF VARANASI

KARMA

Hindus believe that all our actions, including our thoughts, have an effect on us and on other people. The good and bad consequences of our actions are known as karma. Our reincarnation is decided by karma. Bad karma means that the body will be reincarnated as a lower form of life, maybe as an insect. Souls may pass through hundreds of reincarnations before they reach moksha.

VARANASI

Varanasi, on the banks of the River Ganges, is the most sacred city in India. It is sometimes known as Benares. Hindus believe that if they die and are cremated in Varanasi, they will be freed from Samsara.

Many people make a pilgrimage to Varanasi, in the hope of dying there. They are known as Jivan Muktis – those who have been freed while still alive.

SIKHISM

Followers of Sikhism, called Sikhs, believe that death is a step in the journey of life that eventually leads to God. They believe that death is God's will and brings the chance for the soul to return to God. When a Sikh is dying, family and friends gather at their bedside. They say the Sukhmani, the Hymn of Peace. The dying person tries to say 'Waheguru' meaning 'Wonderful Lord'. The dying person may drink amrit, a mixture of sugar and water that has been blessed and stirred with a special sword, called a khanda.

The symbol of the Sikh faith is also called the khanda. Can you spot the double-edged khanda sword in the centre?

PREPARING THE BODY FOR CREMATION

After death, the body is washed and dressed in new clothes by family members. The body is bathed with yoghurt and the hair is covered with a turban or headscarf. The body is wrapped in a white shroud. It is customary for the family to view the prepared body either at home or at the Gurdwara, the Sikh place of worship, before the funeral service.

The Khalsa is a community of Sikhs who have been through a special ceremony and honour Sikh values. The five K's, or articles of faith worn in life, are left with the body when a member of the Khalsa dies. They are: Kara, a steel bracelet; Kachera, a white undergarment; Kirpan, a short sword; Kangha, a wooden comb and Kesh, which is their uncut hair.

THE FUNERAL AND CREMATION

All Sikhs are cremated, rather than being buried. In many parts of the world, the body is carried to the cremation site by relatives. Mourners in the procession sing hymns, called shabads, from the Guru Granth Sahib, the Sikh holy book. They try to remain dignified and not to cry, to show that they accept death as a step towards God. Sweet–smelling, colourful flowers are placed around the body. Sikh funerals can take place at any time, day or night, and Sikhs try to cremate the body within 24 hours of death. Mourners pray that the soul of the dead person will return to God.

Frangipani flowers are used as a symbol that the soul carries on after death.

Before the cremation, either on a funeral pyre or at a crematorium, the Kirtan Sohila is said. This is a Sikh prayer that is said at the end of evening services at the Gurdwara.. If a pyre is used, it is usually lit by a family member, often the eldest son.

A funeral pyre burns fiercely in Jaipur, India.

AFTER THE CREMATION

GURDWARA PATALPURI

After the cremation, the family goes to the Gurdwara or returns to the family home. The Anand Sahib prayer is sung and Ardas, a prayer thanking God and asking for his protection and care, is offered. Karah parshad, a sweet dish made of semolina, flour, sugar and butter, is shared amongst the mourners. The ashes of the dead person may be scattered in flowing water in the sea or a nearby river, or they can be buried in the earth. If possible, Sikhs scatter the ashes at the Gurdwara Patalpuri, which stands on a river bank at Kiratpur.

> The ashes of some of the Gurus who founded Sikhism were scattered on the site of the Gurdwara Patalpuri.

Sikhs believe that, once a person has died and the soul has left, the body is simply an empty shell. For this reason, Sikhs do not erect a gravestone. Although noisy public grieving is not acceptable, Sikhism accepts the sadness of death. Sikhs are expected to grieve privately and to accept comfort and support from the Sikh community. Many families hold a memorial service each year on the anniversary of the death, to remember the dead person.

AKHAND PAATH

The Guru Granth Sahib, compiled by the fifth of the ten Gurus, Arjan, must always be shown great respect.

After the scattering of the ashes, the family arranges Akhand Paath, a continuous reading of the Guru Granth Sahib, from start to finish. It takes 48 hours to complete. Family and friends of the deceased take it in turns to read for two hours at a time. Some families organise a slower reading with breaks, that is timed to finish on the tenth day after the cremation. The reading comforts the bereaved family and friends.

For Sikhs, the oldest male family member is the head of the family. On his death, a new turban may be given to the next oldest male member of the family, symbolising his new responsibilities.

REINCARNATION

Sikhs strongly believe in reincarnation and that the life into which we are reborn is decided by our actions on Earth, or karma. If someone has lived a good life according to the teachings of the Gurus, their soul will reach God and the cycle of birth, death and rebirth will be broken. If not, they will return in human or animal form, as God wishes. Humans are regarded as the highest form of being, and it is only when the soul returns as a human that it has another chance to reach God, by good karma.

BUDDHISM

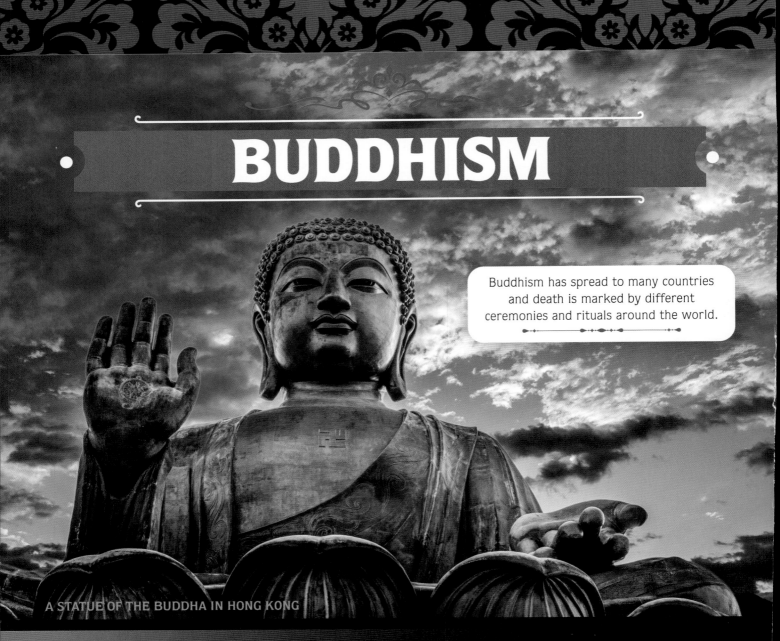

Buddhism has spread to many countries and death is marked by different ceremonies and rituals around the world.

A STATUE OF THE BUDDHA IN HONG KONG

Buddhism was developed in India over 2,500 years ago by a prince, Siddhartha Gautama. He became known as the Buddha, meaning 'Enlightened One', because he reached a state of perfect wisdom and understanding.

All Buddhists believe in a cycle of birth, death and rebirth and that we change in each new life. They believe we have an energy source or consciousness that moves from one life to the next when we die. When a Buddhist is dying, family, friends and monks gather around. They repeat mantras and read from Buddhist teachings. Sometimes, the dying person will try to spend time in quiet thought, called meditation, so that their mind is peaceful. After death, Buddhists try to avoid touching the body for a few days, to allow time for the consciousness to leave. The body is viewed by friends and relatives, who bow to show their respect for the dead person. The time between death and rebirth is known as the bardo state.

In some countries, including Tibet, Mahayana Buddhists believe that the bardo state can last as long as 49 days.

THE FUNERAL

Traditional Buddhist funerals are calm and peaceful. An altar is set up and offerings of flowers and fruit are made. Candles and sweet–smelling incense are lit and gongs or bells are sometimes rung. A photograph of the dead person is displayed, sometimes decorated with flowers.

A TRADITIONAL BUDDHIST FUNERAL IN THAILAND

A TRADITIONAL BUDDHIST FUNERAL PYRE

THE CREMATION OR BURIAL

Buddhism allows people to be buried but most Buddhists are cremated, either at a crematorium or on a traditional funeral pyre.

Each family can decide what to do with the ashes. Some follow the example of the Buddha, whose ashes were buried in structures called stupas. Some scatter the ashes over water.

> The shape of a stupa symbolises the Buddha's enlightenment.

SKY BURIAL

In some places, including Tibet, there is not enough wood to build a pyre and the ground is too hard and rocky for burials. The body is simply left on the side of a mountain and provides food for other animals, including vultures. This is known as a sky burial.

A SKY BURIAL SITE IN CHINA

NIRVANA

The Buddha taught that we always have a choice whether to act selfishly or with kindness and respect. Buddhists believe in reincarnation and that our behaviour in this life affects our next life. The cycle of birth, death and rebirth – Samsara – is only broken when we let go of hatred and greed and reach enlightenment. This state of perfect peace is called nirvana or nibbana.

Although he was born a prince, Siddhartha Gautama gave up his riches, teaching that money and possessions do not bring true happiness.

Some Buddhists mourners meditate and try to do good deeds, which will transfer to the dead person and help them to be reborn into a better life, closer to nirvana. They might, for example, offer food or new robes to the monks.

Mourners offer robes to a monk during a Buddhist funeral in Thailand.

THE LOTUS FLOWER

Buddhists believe that the lotus flower is sacred. Although its roots are in mud, it grows towards the light of the sun, producing a beautiful flower above the muddy water. This symbolises the path that humans should follow towards enlightenment. Lotus flowers are often used in Buddhist funerals, particularly to decorate the coffin.

GLOSSARY

altars	tables used for making offerings to God
amulets	pieces of jewellery, thought to protect the wearer against evil, danger or disease
anointed	rubbed or smeared with oil as part of a religious ceremony
bereaved	having a close friend or relation who has recently died
Book of Psalms	one of the books of the Old Testament in the Bible, containing 150 poems and prayers that can be spoken or sung
coffin	a long, narrow box, usually made of wood, in which a dead body is cremated or buried
confessing	admitting, owning up to
customs	traditional and widely accepted ways of behaving or doing things that are specific to a particular society, place or time
debt	something that is owed, such as money or goods
embalmed	preserved, to prevent or delay the natural decay of a dead body
epitaph	writing on a gravestone, praising and in memory of the dead person
eulogy	a speech given as a tribute at their funeral to someone who has died
grave	a place in a cemetery where a dead person is buried
gravestone	a stone erected over a grave to mark the place of burial
imam	a religious teacher in the Islamic faith
last rites	a religious ceremony performed by a Christian priest for someone close to death
Lord's Prayer	the prayer taught by Jesus to his disciples
mantras	words or phrases repeated many times by people praying or meditating
mourners	people who attend a funeral and feel sadness at the death
organs	parts of the body that have their own specific jobs or functions
plaques	pieces of metal, wood or stone with information inscribed on them
preserved	keep in good condition
prophet	a messenger or teacher of the will of God
pyre	a large pile of wood, used for the cremation of a dead body
rabbi	a teacher of Judaism
Ramadan	the month-long Islamic festival when Muslims do not eat during daylight hours
Sabbath	the Jewish day of rest beginning at nightfall on Friday and ending at nightfall on Saturday
sacred	connected to a god or gods
sarcophagus	a stone coffin, often decorated with painting or sculpture
sari	a piece of clothing made from a single length of cloth draped around the body
shrouds	cloths used to wrap a dead body
sin	a bad act that is seen to be against God's will
souls	the spiritual rather than physical parts of people, considered to live forever
tombs	places for the burial of the dead
traditions	beliefs or behaviours that have been passed down from one generation to the next
undertaker	a person who prepares dead bodies for burial or cremation and arranges funerals
wreath	a ring-shaped arrangement of flowers and leaves, used to decorate a coffin or grave

INDEX

A
afterlife 6–7, 11, 16
amulets 6
angels 9, 12, 19
ashes 13–14, 22, 26–27, 29

B
bells 5, 29
Bible, the 13–14
burials 6–8, 13–14, 16–18, 20–21, 25–26, 29

C
candles 5, 10–11, 18, 29
cemeteries 9, 14, 17–18
ceremonies 4, 8–9, 20, 22, 24, 28
Charon 7
Chevra Kaddisha 8–9
coffins 7, 9, 13–14, 17
cremation 14, 16, 22, 27, 29

D
Day of Judgement 19
death masks 6

E
embalming 6, 8, 13
enlightenment 28–30
epitaphs 14
eulogies 14

F
flowers 4–5, 11, 14–15, 18–20, 25, 29–30
funerals 9–10, 13–18, 21, 24–25, 29

G
Guru Granth Sahib 25, 27

H
hades 7
heaven 5, 12, 15, 19
hell 12, 19
hymns 14, 24–25

I
imams 17

K
karma 23, 27

L
last rites 12

M
moksha 23
mourners 9–10, 14–15, 17–18, 22, 25–26
mummification 6

N
nirvana 30

P
paradise 15, 19
pilgrims 5, 19, 23
prayers 8–12, 14, 17–18, 20–21, 25–26
priests 12–14, 22
pyres 21, 25, 29

Q
Qur'an 19

R
rabbis 9–10
reincarnation 25–27
repentance 12, 15
Resurrection, the 15
rituals 4, 6, 8, 16, 20, 28
rivers 26
 – Ganges 22–23
 – Styx 7

S
samsara 23, 30
samskars 20
shabads 25
shrouds 8–9, 16–17, 24
skulls 5
sky burials 29
souls 5–7, 11–12, 15, 21, 23–27

T
Terracotta Army 7

U
undertakers 13

V
Varanasi 23

W
wreaths 7

PHOTO CREDITS

Front Cover – Kzenon. 2 – Konstantin Tronin. 4 – Kzenon, EQRoy. 5 – AGCuesta, Anton_Ivanov, hikrcn. 6 – rocharibeiro, pgaborphotos, Paul Fleet, francesco de marco. 7 – DnDavis. 8 – maratr. 9 – meunierd. 10 – Binh Thanh Bui, Gamzova Olga. 11 – Kletr, James.Pintar. 12 – Marc Bruxelle, Gina Vescovi. 13 – By Art Konovalov. 14 – Robert Hoetink, a katz, douglasmack. 15 – Fresnel, Everett Historical. 16 – Ba dins, Alexandru Nika. 17 – Northfoto, Asianet–Pakistan. 18 – Zurijeta. 19 – kamomeen, Farris Noorzali. 20 – espies, Dmitry Kalinovsky. 21 – Alisa24, RPBaiao. 22 – MoLarjung, Claudine Van Massenhove. 23 – milosk50. 24 – Viktorija Reuta. 25 – MISS KANITHAR AIUMLA–OR, StanislavBeloglazov. 26 – Wikipedia. 27 – Tukaram.Karve. 28 – NikomMaelao Production, Tamonwan_Newnew, Andaman, beibaoke. 29 – Pavel L Photo and Video, I AM NIKOM. 30 – ANURAKE SINGTO–ON, cooperr. Border on all pages: PremiumVector.